I0235100

IMAGES
of America

MANALAPAN
AND
ENGLISHTOWN

This is an 1873 Beers' Atlas map of Manalapan Township.

MANALAPAN

Scale 60 Rods to the inch

Manalapan Township.
Business Notices.

IMAGES
of America

MANALAPAN
AND
ENGLISHTOWN

Richard J. Dalik

ARCADIA
PUBLISHING

Copyright © 1998 by Richard J. Dalik
ISBN 978-1-5316-6062-8

Published by Arcadia Publishing
Charleston, South Carolina

For all general information contact Arcadia Publishing at:
Telephone 843-853-2070
Fax 843-853-0044
E-mail sales@arcadiapublishing.com
For customer service and orders:
Toll-Free 1-888-313-2665

Visit us on the Internet at www.arcadiapublishing.com

Contents

Acknowledgments

I would like to thank each and every person who gave of their time and effort to help make this book possible. A special thanks goes to my wife, Sally, whose dedication to the cause, patience, and typing skills made this project attainable. Lydia Wikoff, a charter member of the Battleground Historical Society and Manalapan Township historian, provided family photographs as well as early township views. She answered our questions and assisted with research. Battleground Historical Society Treasurer Jane Zdancewic, also a charter member, shared family albums and was a great help in identifying the many early homes that appear in this book. Dorothy McCue, a member of the society, spent many hours helping us find the right words to describe our images. Former BHS President Ed Burke Jr., along with his father, provided family photographs and shared stories. Dr. Gary Stone, Historic Preservation Specialist, wrote the text for the Revolutionary War portion of the Military History chapter. Other BHS members—Constance Dreyer, Nancy DuBois Wood, Mary Ker, John McDonald, Doris Perrine, Randy Rauscher, Jennie Salter, and Margaret Weber—provided photographs and information to support our efforts to document local history. Longtime residents of Englishtown, Manalapan Township, and Freehold—Percy Bloom; Pauline Carr; Doris Clayton; Fred Davis; Alma Grove; David Jasper; Ted Narozanick; Izabella Orr; Taylor, June, and Heather Palmer; Bernice Rue; and Olga Ulatowski—furnished images and knowledge. Our friends, Henry Cross, Bob Goldfine, and Glenn Vogel, gave us encouragement and moral support.

Introduction

The rich land of western Monmouth County that is now Manalapan Township and Englishtown Boro was originally part of Freehold Township. The village of Englishtown can be traced back to the early 1700s and was incorporated as Englishtown Boro in 1888. Manalapan Township was established in 1848 when Freehold Township was divided. Manalapan will celebrate its 150th year in 1998.

The name Manalapan is derived from the Indian words meaning "good bread" and "good land." The village of Englishtown received its name from James English, a proprietor of the land and an original settler. Englishtown was the commercial center for exporting agricultural products, and Manalapan was the major farming community. The farms figured significantly in the development of the surrounding villages, which became thriving trading and commercial centers with mills, blacksmith shops, and taverns.

In the 18th century, the community tavern constituted the heart of the village. Citizens gathered there for discussions about local political issues, which often led to heated exchanges about political unrest in the colonies. These gatherings sparked the early fire of discontent, which resulted in the burning desire for freedom. This outcry for political freedom became a common thread in the tapestry of discontent throughout the colonies, eventually resulting in the Revolutionary War. The Village Inn, an old tavern in Englishtown, was a place for local residents to voice their feelings during this volatile time in our country's history.

The Revolutionary War has particular significance for Manalapan and Englishtown since an important battle of the war, the Battle of Monmouth, was fought on the farmlands of the region. Several views in this book depict the arena of the battle as well as some prominent edifices of historical importance. The inspiration for this book originated with the Battleground Historical Society, a group comprised of concerned local citizens who have restored the Village Inn, which dates back to the early 18th century. The Battleground Historical Society's purpose in compiling this book is to preserve the history of a thriving agricultural community which, during the past few years, has been transformed dramatically from fertile, productive farmlands to modern housing developments.

The photographs and postcards included in this book have been gathered from three primary sources: a 1970s house-marking project of the Battleground Historical Society, postcards from the author's collection, and photographs from the private collections and albums of members of the society and interested local residents.

The visual images in this book are not intended to cover the complete history of the Manalapan and Englishtown area, but are an attempt to present a glimpse of life in these communities in the late 19th and early 20th centuries. While the Battleground Historical Society has a strong commitment to preserve the history of the area for future generations, it is our hope that this book will also bring great enjoyment to its readers.

ENGLISHTOWN

MANALAPAN TSP.

Scale 30 Rods to the Inch

Englishtown
Business Notices

Anderson I. E..Manufr, New York. Res., Main St
Applegate A. T. (M. D.)..Physician and Surgeon, Office, Main St
Besthoff Solomon..Dealer in Dry Goods, Groceries, Boots and Shoes, Hats and Caps, Hardware, Crockery and Glass Ware, Liquors and Cigars, Main St
Dey B. V..Mason and Builder and Farmer, Main St
Forman Garret..Manufr and Dealer in Harness, Flynets, Whips, &c. Justice of the Peace, Water St.
Jewell J. L..Manufr Carriages, Buggies, &c. Jobbing and Repairing, near Station
Laird John H..Dealer in Dry Goods and Groceries, Clothing, Hats and Caps, Boots and Shoes, Carpets and Oil Cloths, Hardware, Woodenware and Crockery, Liquors, Drugs, Paints and Oils, Flour and Grain, Coal and Wood, Lime and Cement, Agricultural Implements, Plows and Castings, Cucumber Pumps, Hay Rope and Hay Wire, Field and Garden Seeds, Wool Dealer, Main St
Lustig Joseph..Tanner and Currier and Wool Puller' Dealer in Hides, Skins, Wool and Fur, Water St. Office, 68 Cliff St., N. Y.
Murray Robt. W..Manufr and Dealer in Harness, Flynets, Whips, &c., and Carriage Trimmer, Main St

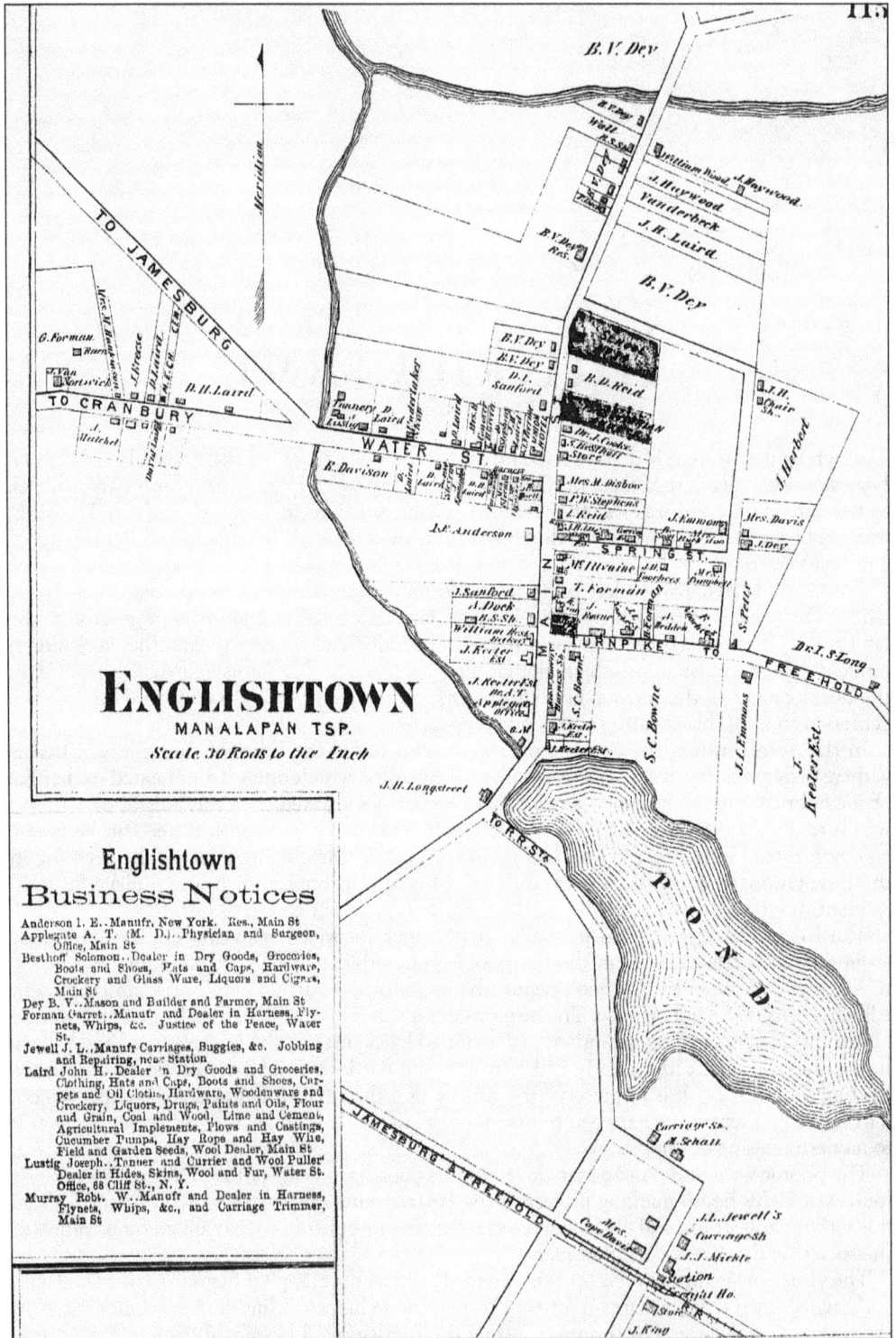

This is an 1873 *Beers' Atlas* map of Englishtown.

One

Englishtown

Although normally a thriving business center, Main Street was captured by this photographer during a tranquil moment on a Sunday afternoon. Looking south, William E. Mount's General Merchandise Store is the first building on the left in this 1906 postcard. Later this building was occupied by Addison & Arnold, a hardware and farm supply store. Today it is Rick's Saddle Shop.

On September 2, 1904, William E. Mount was granted the first franchise to sell Ford automobiles in the state of New Jersey. Soon after, an ad in the Freehold Transcript offered a free demonstration to intending purchasers. The 1904 model had a 10-horsepower engine capable of speeds up to 30 or 35 miles per hour and sold for $800. Two cars were sold in 1904. By 1916, sales had increased dramatically and 933 cars were sold.

Local farmers would swap butter, eggs, and produce for canned goods, fabrics, and hardware. This August 2, 1902 bill shows the account of J. Van McElvaine, who purchased wire, washboard, fruit, and other items over a period of time, and received $10 credit for 5 bushels of potatoes on April 17.

Cars are parked on Main Street, looking south. In front of Mount's store on the left there is an early gas pump, *c.* 1915. The first store on the right is Clayton Palmer's butcher shop.

This *c.* 1890 image shows Thomas Burtt's general store and insurance business on Main Street near the corner of Water Street. At this time the store also served as the post office.

Here we see Main Street looking north *c.* 1910. The first store on the right is the Hamilton Drug Store, followed by Nate Vanderveer's house and Vandenberg's General Merchandise Store. On the left is the Hotel Central.

Mr. C. Oppermann Jr., proprietor of the Hotel Central, is on the left in this *c.* 1915 postcard. Later the building was made into two stores. One side was occupied by the American Store Company. The other side housed a confectionery store, whose owners included Farrel Smith and later Joe Eisenberg. The building is no longer standing.

Main Street, looking South, Englishtown, N. J.

The First National Bank of Englishtown is on the right in this 1910 street scene. The building immediately south of the bank was divided into two stores, with living quarters above. Next to the bank was a butcher shop owned by David Richmond, and later Clayton Palmer. The other side housed a small general store operated by Mr. and Mrs. Barber, who owned the building. At this time the post office was across the street, next to Frank Lewis's ice cream shop.

The Hulse Memorial Home at 25 Main Street, shown in 1913, was originally built as a tavern by Moses Laird in the 18th century. Later owners included J.H. Laird, William E. Mount, and J. Laird Hulse, who made the building into a funeral parlor about 1926. The Victorian home next door was Dr. Anderson's house and office, now Fancy Flowers.

13

The Applegate Engine & Hose Company was organized in June of 1904. William E. Mount was the first president. The borough bought the property, located on the corner of Main Street and Tennent Avenue, from Nicholas McDonald and constructed the firehouse as it appears in this 1906 postcard. It was reorganized in 1914 as The Englishtown Fire Company.

APPLEGATE ENGINE AND HOSE COMPANY—ENGLISHTOWN, N. J.

This newspaper photograph was taken *c.* 1910. Members of the Applegate Engine & Hose Company gathered in full dress to celebrate a patriotic holiday. Marching with them is the Washington Field Drum Corps from Perth Amboy. Among the members are Chief Con Oppermann, Roy Applegate, James Lutes, Samuel Burke, Jacob Trautman, Frank Laird, Clayton Palmer, John Kirkland, Charles Reed, William Hess, and Driver Alonzo Dunfee. Uncle Sam is portrayed by E. Vought Burke, a local resident who was famous for being 7 feet tall. He appeared in numerous Monmouth County parades and his services were always in demand.

The municipal building, shown here c. 1825, was originally a tavern operated by Stephen Abrams and his son Simon. It was later operated as a tavern and a bakery by William Hess. The borough purchased the property on April 6, 1920, to use for offices and a firehouse. The municipal offices are now located next door in the former post office building. The fire department has a new building on Iron Ore Road.

Council President Taylor Palmer left no doubt in the minds of the borough's populace as to his brand of politics when he rode to the polls astride a white mule in 1935. Palmer started from his home on Railroad Avenue to ride his Democratic mount to the firehouse polling place, three blocks distant. He was later mayor from January 1942 to December 31, 1944.

Dr. Asher T. Applegate started his practice of medicine on Wednesday, April 19, 1871. His first office was in an upstairs room that he rented in this house located at 11 Main Street. After marriage in 1873 to Miss Jennie C. Wilson, he bought the property and the couple lived here. A real country doctor, Applegate made house calls by horse and buggy and he always used a driver. One of his first drivers was James Christie, who had a blacksmith shop. When Ford cars became available, the doctor bought a coupe and was driven by his son James.

Dr. Applegate was a well-loved and active member of the community. He was the first mayor of Englishtown and a member of Knights of Pythias Lodge and the Masons. This bill of $19 for medical services rendered to the McElvaine family covered a two-year period. A handwritten thank-you shows his personal touch and the sincere concern he had for his patients.

At a sheriff's sale in 1899, Dr. Applegate purchased the property at 12 Main Street, which included the house and land shown on the left in this 1909 postcard. He lived here and had his office at this location for many years.

Dr. Applegate's property extended to Tennent Avenue, where he created a beautiful lawn containing many unusual trees, flowers, and shrubs. The windmill was a familiar landmark in the borough. The Sovereign Bank and Jack Frost Luncheonette are now located on the site.

The residence of Dr. Asher T. Applegate, the first mayor of Englishtown (1896–1932), later became the home of the Hamilton family. The home is shown here in a *c.* 1912 postcard view. In 1976, a daughter, Edna Hamilton, became the first woman mayor in the borough. The house was built by Robert Murray of Freehold in 1836 and he operated a harness shop on the property.

Another daughter, Vera Hamilton, posed for the photographer with her teddy bear *c.* 1907.

The Woodruff House at 7 Main Street, built *c.* 1830, is located on the mill property owned by Jacob Keeler in 1850. In 1927 Dr. Applegate bought the property and lived there until his death in 1932. Dr. Ralph Woodruff began his practice in Englishtown in December of 1931 and later purchased this house from the Applegate Estate. He continued to serve his patients until he retired in 1979. Many local residents in the area were brought into the world by these dedicated physicians. The house is now an antique shop.

The power plant located next to the Woodruff property was formerly a gristmill. The Manalapan Light Co. purchased the mill in 1905. It became the Freehold and Jamesburg Light Co. in 1911 and provided electrical power to Englishtown and surrounding communities. The old mill was destroyed by fire in 1922.

At the turn of the century the Englishtown Millpond was a favorite spot for young people to show off their skating skills. It also provided ice for the preservation of food.

The home of Charles F. McDonald Sr., who served as a Democratic state committeeman, is located at 48 Main Street. It was formerly the office of Dr. J. Cook. It was later occupied by McDonald's son, Charles Jr., and currently by his grandson John. The Presbyterian church is adjacent to the property.

North Main Street, Englishtown, N. J.

This image looks south on Main Street *c.* 1910. The first house at 49 Main Street was owned by the Laird family and later by Joseph Noce, who was the manager of the local American Store. Roman Catholic services were held here before the church was built. The second house at 47 Main Street was owned by William N. Steward, who operated a hay press near the railroad station. The house was later purchased by Edward Rooney, co-owner of Rooney & Ely.

This view looks south on Main Street approaching the bridge over McGelliard's Brook *c.* 1920. Eleanor Snyder Griswold, a local schoolteacher, lived in the small bungalow on the left. The Burke family homestead is in the distance. It was later the home of Harry Thompson.

This originally was a one-and-one-half-story building used by Robert Newell as his home and a tailor shop c. 1726. During the mid-18th century the Davis family, Thomas and his son Moses, operated a tavern in the building. The business continued as a tavern with many different owners who made structural changes. In the early 1870s it was known as the Union Hotel under the direction of John J. Perrine. The Fleming family purchased the property in 1879 and it became the Village House. Shown in this c. 1880 photograph from left to right are John Perrine, John West (bartender), Craig Fleming (proprietor), Richard Fleming (Craig's father), Gilbert Hulse (local undertaker), and Jacob Trautman Sr. (barber). Margaret Reid Fleming, Craig's wife, is looking out the window.

A familiar landmark in Englishtown, the Village Inn was inherited by Hazel Fleming Applegate, wife of James T. Applegate, the son of Dr. Asher T. Applegate. During Prohibition the Inn served as a tea room and later was re-established as a tavern and popular restaurant, primarily due to the culinary skills of the cook, John Perrine Sr. It is now owned by the Battleground Historical Society, which has restored this significant historic site.

Abraham Perrine brought passengers from the railroad station to the Village Inn in this early coach.

Water Street, West from Main, Englishtown, N. J

This is Water Street in 1912. The first building on the left was the home of Howard Davison. Mike Gibbs had a shoe repair shop in his house next door.

On Water Street, looking east towards Main Street, the first house on the right was the home of Gilbert Hulse, an undertaker. Note the carriage step at the curb.

Maude Rogers, local postmistress, lived in the first house on the left, which was built by Frank Lewis. Christie's Confectionery Store was located in the next building, immediately before the Village Inn. The structure facing Water Street housed a barbershop on the right side that was owned and operated by Jake Trautman Sr. and Jake Trautman Jr. A billiard parlor was on the left side.

The Knights of Pythias, Columbia Lodge 88, was chartered on July 7, 1873, with 17 members. The first meetings were held in the local schoolhouse. In 1880 the membership had grown to 61 men and occupied the second story of Trautman's barbershop. The Columbia Hall pictured here was built in 1891. Meetings were held on the second floor, and the first floor was rented for movies, dances, weddings, and other local functions. Marion Rhoades Freeman played the piano for the movies run by George L. Vandenberg and Forman Rhoades. Dances were run by Edward Woodward, Charles Nowack, Taylor Palmer, and Wilson McBride.

This view looks east on Tennent Avenue—formerly Church Street—c. 1916. The first house on the right was owned by Sam Ely, co-owner of Rooney & Ely.

Here we look west on Tennent Avenue approaching the town of Englishtown. The home of Mr. Bortner, superintendent of schools for Manalapan Township, is visible.

As one entered the town from the station on Railroad Avenue in 1917, he would pass Dorey Hann's basket factory on the left and approach the VanDorn farm and livery.

A 1905 postcard shows passengers waiting for the train after purchasing a ticket from Charles Reed, the local ticket master. On Sundays in the summertime as many as 300 tourists would take the train back to the city. They would travel west through Jamesburg, the Amboys, and Newark before reaching New York City.

A train is pulling into the Englishtown railroad station to deliver passengers and freight *c.* 1906. From here, continuing east, the train would stop at Tennent and Freehold.

In 1914, freight as well as passengers arrived at the Englishtown railroad station. Ford cars were shipped to the William Mount agency in railroad boxcars. The chassis were packed in crates without wheels, bodies, tops, or fenders. When they arrived at the station, wheels were put on, gas was put in a tank under the front seat, and drivers would take them to Mr. Mount's garage, where assembly was completed.

A humorous greeting was sent home c. 1915 while the sender was vacationing in Englishtown. Penny postcards were available at the general store.

Looking across Main Street from the alley between the municipal building and Frueh Bros. Garage, one can see the Willy's-Knight Automobile Agency and repair shop, owned by J. Laird Hulse c. 1930. This location was later the site of Gelber's Grocery Store and Narozanick's hardware store.

John and Bill Frueh opened Frueh Bros. Garage at 15 Main Street about 1928. In addition to providing gas and auto repairs, the Frueh brothers operated a small Chevrolet dealership here for a short time. This 1935 view shows the tow truck, Esso gas pumps, and glass oil bottles. The station was replaced by a modern post office c. 1965, and it is now the borough hall.

Gus Grevsen owned and operated a garage and machine shop at 70 Tennent Avenue for many years. In this mid-30s image Gus is giving directions to a passing motorist. Note that Blue Sunoco gas was 18.9¢ per gallon. This is now the site of the Citgo service station owned by Frank Ulatowski Jr.

Bloom Bros. Garage was established on Water Street in 1934 by four brothers, Perry, Robert, Oscar, and Marty. A 1939 photograph shows the Cities Service gas pumps located right at the curb and early Coca-Cola advertising signs. The business continued until 1979.

Members of the Englishtown Lions Club Community Band pause in front of the American Legion on Sanford Street before marching in a Memorial Day parade. James Mate, a music teacher at the Englishtown Public School, was the band director.

The Englishtown and Manalapan Township First Aid Squad was formed in the late 1930s. In 1941 the charter members posed with their first ambulance. From left to right are as follows: (front row) Happy Whelan, Duncan Perrine, Arthur Robbins, Lester Hann, George Geunsch, and Harry Burke; (back row) Ray Lemmings, Bill Eckman, Fred Conover, Bob Noce, Charles Errickson, Bob Vandenberg, Walter Noce, and Dick Schwartz.

Two

Tennent and Surrounding Villages

The original toll road leading to the village of Tennent—Patten's Corner and Manalapan Turnpike—passed the Old Tennent Church and cemetery, as seen in this c. 1926 view. Rev. William Tennent, the pastor for 43 years, was so loved by his congregation and members of the community that both the church and the village were named for him. Traveling on Tennent Road, west of the old road, you can still see the monument erected in 1920 in memory of the soldiers and sailors who gave their lives in World War I.

Looking north on Tennent Road from the intersection of Craig Road, William and Caroline McGantlin leave their farmhouse to attend services at the Old Tennent Church c. 1910.

Approaching the intersection of Tennent Road and Freehold-Englishtown Road, the Sutphen home and blacksmith shop are on the left. The Tennent Post Office is now located on the site.

A 1910 postcard view looking west on the Freehold-Englishtown Road shows the Callahan farm on the right. The property is now Roth's Farm Nursery across from the Old Silver Tavern.

The Tennent Post Office was located in this general store on Main Street c. 1910. The property now provides an entrance to the current post office.

A. Merriman, a Howell Township photographer, took many photographs of Tennent and surrounding villages c. 1910, including this one of the home of Ephriam Laird on Main Street.

John Laird, son of Ephriam, lived in this Victorian home on Main Street. It was later used by the New Jersey State Police as their Manalapan headquarters.

In 1910 Ephriam Laird served the local residents at his general store next to the railroad station on Main Street. A hardware store was added and his son John continued the business.

This rare view of the Tennent railroad station shows a small building that served passengers as well as farmers who shipped their produce to market. Local students used the railroad to travel to Freehold High School, while others commuted to college in the Trenton area.

The Monmouth County Farmers Exchange was a local co-op owned by farmers to provide wholesale distribution of farm products. It also provided farmers with an opportunity to purchase their supplies at a reduced price. This small branch office was located across the street from the railroad station c. 1912. The team of horses is pulling a dump cart used to carry gravel for road maintenance.

Potatoes were transferred from barrels to burlap bags for loading into the Pennsylvania Railroad freight cars behind the Monmouth County Farmers Exchange office, as shown in this 1910 photo card. One barrel equaled one bag, and these weighed approximately 150 pounds each.

At the height of the season c. 1922, bags of potatoes are stacked at the warehouse of John M. Laird in Tennent, ready for shipment to various markets.

John M. Laird is standing in front of his farm equipment business in 1939. This building was later occupied by Burke's Pumps.

George Huff's Blacksmith and Wheelright Shop was located at Rue's Corner—the intersection of Main Street, Millhurst Road, and Woodward Road—in Tennent *c.* 1910.

From left to right, Gloria DuBois, Thomas Bums, Fred DuBois Jr., Doris Pulaski, Carl Summerbell, and William Pulaski are playing on the rye stacks at Reed & Perrine's *c.* 1931.

Rue's Garage, situated on the northeast corner of Tennent Road and the Freehold-Englishtown Road, opened in May of 1939 and sold Esso gasoline, now Exxon. The business continued for 29 years, and is now Serafin's Service Center. Early outdoor restrooms are on the right.

Bill McGee's Old Tennent Service across the street sold Gulf gasoline c. 1945. Mr. McGee also opened a small general store on the left. It is now the Battleground Deli and the gas station is the location of the current Tennent Post Office.

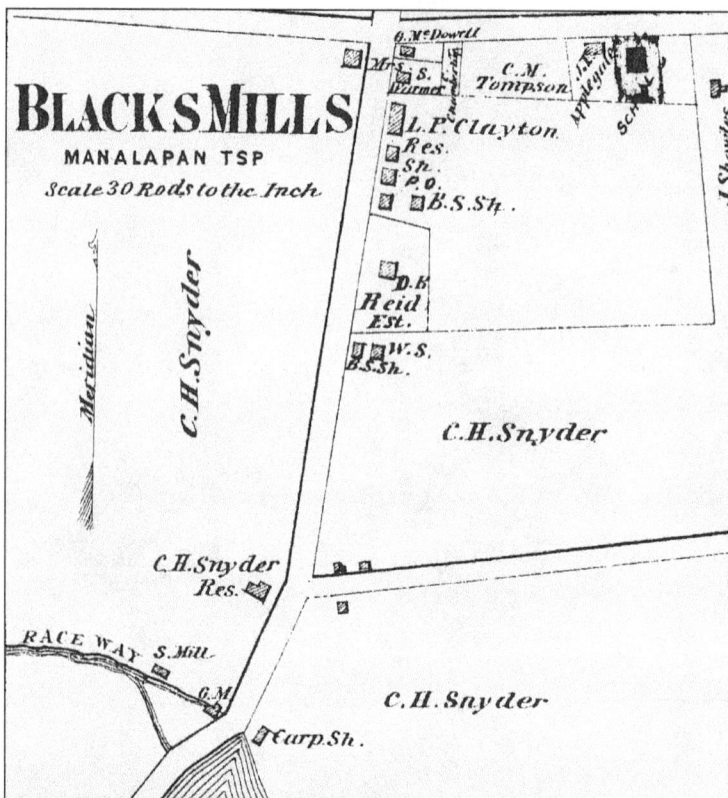

This map of Blacks Mills, now Millhurst, from the 1873 *Beers' Atlas* shows the C.H. Snyder property surrounding his gristmill.

In a 1910 postcard view taken from Route 33, a small group of homes and a general store are located on Millhurst Road leading to the mill.

Another view shows Millhurst Road as it crosses the dam and the spillway, which provided waterpower to the mill.

The millpond also was a source of recreational opportunities—such as boating, fishing, and swimming—for nearby residents.

The Smithburg area of Manalapan Township appears in an 1873 *Beers' Atlas* map. It borders Millstone and Freehold Townships and was formerly known as Smithville. An early tavern operated by the Smith family, later known as the Parker house, is listed as the Smithville Hotel. Joel Parker, governor of New Jersey from 1863 to 1866 and again from 1872 to 1875, was born in this house.

The Smithburg millpond was a favorite place to fish. A message from Hazel on the back of this postcard tells her friend Margaret, "I am going fishing and I might bring one home for you to cook!" Note the water lilies in the foreground.

The photographer, A. Merriman, left his car parked in front of the Smithburg General Store as he took a photograph of the owner, William A. Homer, and his friends. A sign on the left reads "Use Dr. A.C. Daniels' Horse and Dog Medicines for home treatment. Sold here."

In 1894 William and John B. Parker owned and operated the general store at Smithburg. They also were dealers in marl and pine boards. Marl was a composition derived from fossil remains and was discovered in the area by an Irish workman in the 18th century. As a natural form of fertilizer, marl became an important commodity for the farmers because it improved the soil and increased productivity.

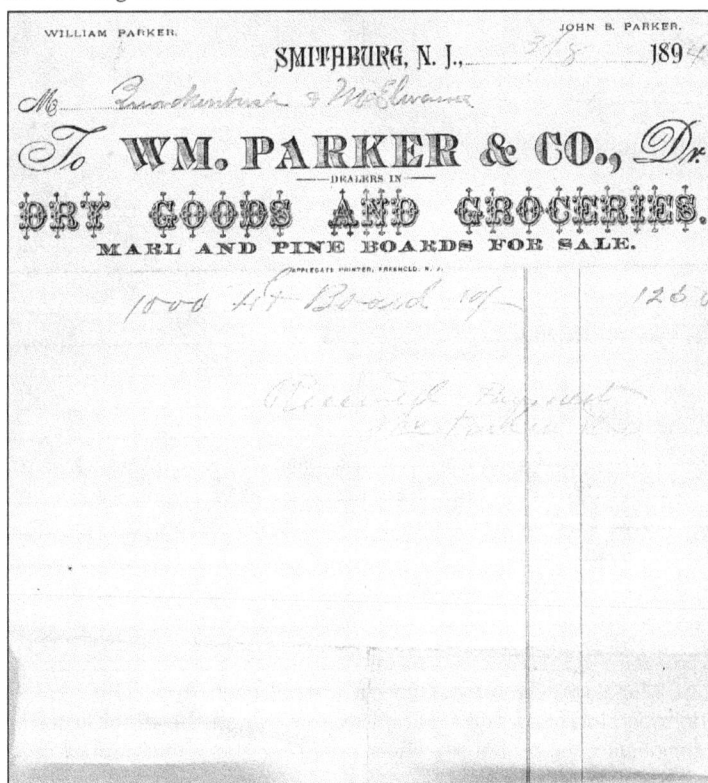

The village of Manalapan was located on the Hightstown and Manalapan Turnpike (Route 33) near the intersection with the Manalapan-Englishtown Turnpike (Route 527A). An early postcard shows the general store and post office on the left. The Manalapan Hotel is in the background. These buildings are no longer standing.

The Manalapan Hotel was an early stagecoach stop. The 1873 *Beers' Atlas* lists it as Capt. Mount's Hotel. By 1889, H.S. Davison owned the hotel according to Wolverton's *Atlas of Monmouth County*. Later owners posed for the photographer *c.* 1912 as flowers bloomed in boxes on the porch roof.

Three

Farming and Rural Life

An inscription on the front of a 1915 postcard indicates that Monmouth County's "fertile potato fields control the market of the United States." On the Forman Stillwell farm located on Route 9 north of Pine Brook Road, workers are harvesting potatoes into baskets, which will later be transferred to barrels for transportation to the local freight station.

A mule team driven by Bill Reid leaves the Reid farm on Craig Road with a wagonload of potatoes on its way to Tennent about 1915.

Wagons were specially designed locally to hold 16 barrels for transportation of potatoes from the field to the train station. Barrels of potatoes were then dumped on a conveyor belt and put into burlap bags for shipping. This photograph was taken c. 1920.

A familiar late summer scene in 1919 featured potatoes being sorted and bagged at Reed & Perrine's in Tennent.

Reed & Perrine drivers pose with their Ford trucks before beginning a day of deliveries to local farmers c. 1935. The first man on left is Chris Errickson and the second man on the left is Frank Jeffrey.

In 1928 Leon and Stella Zdancewic were busy sorting cucumbers to sell at the local market in Freehold. The baskets were also used to hold 50 ears of corn that were sold at the market. The Zdancewics traveled from their farm on the Freehold-Smithburg Road in a GMC truck at a top speed of 18 miles per hour on the dirt road into Freehold.

Stella Zdancewic and her friend Harriet are milking the family cow, "Red." Many households had at least one cow to provide the family with milk, butter, and cheese.

In the 1920s, Walter Tylenda brought a load of hay into the barn on the Zdancewic farm, later known as Wood-Z-Lane Farm. Next to the load of hay is a grain reaper.

This steam engine was being pulled into the field by horses in order to run the thrasher, which separated the grain from the sheaves. The stack would be raised when the engine was started. Enoch Burke, a Tennent farmer, is on the far left. He rented the steam engine, which was a common practice in the 1890s.

J. Chalmers Rue, a Tennent farmer, received a patent in 1872 to manufacture a plow that became known as the "Famous Rue Plow" around the turn of the century.

Jesse Boyce is seen driving the McCormick reaper on what is now the Charles Wikoff farm on Tennent Road, near Gordons Corner. Boyce operated the reaper c. 1926 to harvest rye.

A blacksmith was a very important member of the community since the farmers relied upon him for his skills. John Morrell Hampton operated his shop at Gordons Corner at the turn of the century. It is now the site of a chiropractic center.

T.S. Fox was a local carriage and wagon builder on the corner of Route 33 and Millhurst Road c. 1905.

Taylor Palmer Sr. is ready to serve customers in a small-town butcher shop c. 1924. He used a Steiner meat grinder, wooden butcher-block tables, a Dayton scale, and a National cash register. Sawdust was always found on the floor of a butcher shop.

The first tractor used on the Wood-Z-Lane Farm was a 1936 John Deere purchased at Addison & Arnold in Englishtown. This was the last model made with steel rims. In 1939 Pete Zdancewic and his friends were having a little fun before getting the fields ready for planting.

Charles Wikoff prepares for a day of work on a later-model John Deere tractor purchased from the showroom at Addison & Arnold in 1949.

Stanley Boyce drives the Oliver tractor on his farm on Craig Road with helper Martin VanSiclen c. 1948. Stanley's son Alan is getting a free ride.

ENGLISHTOWN AUCTION SALES
SALES EVERY SATURDAY
PHONE 4822-ENGLISHTOWN, N.J.

Photo by BILL M

ENGLISHTOWN AUCTION SALES

STEVE'S MAIN BROOK INN BAR & RESTAURANT

Englishtown Auction Sales has been a landmark in Manalapan Township for almost 70 years. It began in 1929 as a livestock market where farmers sold their produce and used farm equipment. In 1945 the concept expanded to include retail auctioneering. Today it is known as a bargain hunter's paradise for new and used merchandise.

Steve and Katie Sobecko, founders of Englishtown Auction Sales, are pictured here in front of their Main Brook Inn in 1929.

William M. Taylor and George S. Kincaid came to Manalapan Township from North Port, Long Island, in 1925 and began a wholesale florist business on Route 33 near Millhurst. At the start, they grew only carnations in one greenhouse. An aerial view shows how the business expanded to become a large wholesale and retail facility by 1954. The furnace used 1 ton of coal a night, which was shoveled by hand, until the fueling system was switched to a 20,000-gallon oil tank in 1947. William's son, Elbert M. Taylor, purchased the Kincaid interest in 1946 and continued in operation until 1982.

Before 1805 a distillery was built by Elisha Combs on Wemrock Brook (Route 33). It was later purchased by James A. Perrine, who added a gristmill at the same location in 1866. Only the gristmill is shown in this c. 1955 photograph. The property is now part of the Monmouth Battlefield State Park and the buildings are gone.

An impressive bill head on this invoice dated January 23, 1908, includes a photograph of the early distillery building. A gallon of apple brandy cost $2 in 1894.

58

Blacks Mills (Millhurst) was named for John Black, who operated a sawmill and gristmill on the Manalapan Brook from 1813 to 1837. The property was sold in 1859 to Charles H. Snyder, who enlarged the gristmill and added machinery for making flour. This mill's capacity grew to 75 barrels of flour in 24 hours. It was purchased by the Millhurst Milling Company in 1925, and that company continued to operate the mill until the mid-1940s. The building remains standing on the site.

The Smithburg Mill was built by William Preston c. 1800 on Manalapan Brook (1 mile north of Route 537 on Route 527A) as a woolen mill. It was sold to Asher Smith c. 1844, at which time it had a pair of carding machines and 50 spindles. The village of Smithville, later Smithburg, was named after Asher Smith. Robert S. Blain later owned the mill from 1866 to 1889. The mill is no longer standing.

The Joseph Taylor Farm was situated on Taylor Mills Road near McGelliard's Brook at a very old mill site. It was purchased by the Taylor family in 1877, and this family rebuilt the mill to use the roller process of flouring. The mill and the pond are no longer there.

A view of Taylor's Mill c. 1895 shows workers loading bags of flour into wagons for delivery. The advertising on the wagons reads "Jos. W. Taylor's Roller Flouring Mills, Englishtown, N. J." A sawmill was also located on the property to provide lumber for the local community.

A December 5, 1906 Gross Bros. bill head indicates that these brothers succeeded the Taylor family in the ownership of the mill. Did Cream of Wheat originate in Manalapan Township?

Additional locations are listed on a later Gross Bros. bill head, indicating the business's expansion.

Bergen Mills, shown on this *c.* 1910 photo card, served the area known as Manalapan in the western part of the township.

The mill located on Weamaconk Pond in the village of Englishtown dates back to Revolutionary times; it was known as Sharp's Mill in 1779. At the "Old Red Mill," Jacob Keeler was an active, well-known miller *c.* 1850. Farmers bartered for milling services in exchange for mill products. Later owners were Charles VanCleef and William Parker.

The famous Rhea Chair on display at the Monmouth County Historical Association in Freehold was made in 1695 by Robert Rhea, a carpenter. The Rhea farm, located in Manalapan and Freehold Townships, encompassed portions of the Monmouth Battlefield State Park. The Rhea family came from Scotland in 1688 and the Scottish influence is shown in the detailed carving. It is said to be the oldest documented chair in the state.

The spear-back, rush-bottom chair made by Pierson Thompson—who lived near the railroad station in the village of Englishtown c. 1840s—also had bent rear posts. In 1853 Thompson died at the age of 52 and is buried at the Old Tennent Church cemetery.

John Leonard, an apprentice, continued Pierson Thompson's business after his death, and later built his own shop and home at Rue's Corner in Tennent. He cut maple for chair posts and oak for rounds from his own wood lot. His son Peter started working with him at age 12, and in 1867 received board, lodging, and $15 a month. This three-slat, bent-back, rush-bottom chair, c. 1855, originally sold for $1.50.

J. Davidson Herbert was the son of James C. Herbert, who had a chair shop located on the corner of Pine Street and Harrison Avenue in Englishtown, and he worked for his father and later for John Leonard. After he was discharged from the Civil War, he opened his own chair shop on LaSatta Avenue about 1866. Herbert's favorite stencil patterns for the wide-top slat of his chairs incorporated peaches and pears.

Four

Family and Friends

The Stillwell family gathered in front of the family homestead in 1880, posing for a local photographer. Forman Stillwell shows off his prize horse, while his wife, Mary Smock Stillwell, and her sister are dressed in their Sunday best. Forman's father, Joseph Stillwell, bought the homestead located near Gordons Corner in 1839 when he came from Shrewsbury. His son Forman inherited the farm in 1858 upon the death of his father. The house was demolished about 1939 when Route 9 was built.

George Stillwell, son of Forman Stillwell, is shown about 1900 with his dog "Guess" in front of his homestead near Gordons Corner, known as Killdee Farm. The house is located on what is currently Route 9 and is presently a real estate office. On May 7, 1980, George Stillwell's granddaughter, Lydia Wikoff, was presented with a Century Farm Award by the New Jersey Agricultural Society commemorating seven generations of the Stillwell family living on the farm. Her sons, Charles III and James, currently farm the property with their father, Charles Wikoff Jr.

Three generations gather on the porch of the George Stillwell homestead in 1903 after church on Sunday. George's son, Oliver K. Stillwell, is on the left in the front row. George's son, Staats Stillwell, and his wife, Florence Conover Stillwell (with dog), are on the right.

Staats Stillwell and his wife, Florence, are shown in front of the Conover homestead on Gordons Corner Road in 1924 preparing to take a leisurely Sunday afternoon buggy ride.

Florence Conover Stillwell enjoys a cool refreshment on a hot summer day on the Conover farm c. 1915.

Oliver Stillwell, son of George, married Grace Hodapp in Spotswood, New Jersey, in 1912 and later settled on the Stillwell homestead at Gordons Corner. The couple raised three children: Hamilton, Eleanor, and Lydia.

To the far right are Grace and Oliver Stillwell's children, Eleanor and Hamilton. The two are joined their Appleby cousins, Betty (far left), Ted (second from left), and Bud (center), for a birthday party. Eleanor Stillwell must see the cake arriving aglow with candles!

In 1918 Grace Stillwell is feeding chickens in front of the Sutphen-Herbert house located on the Battlefield State Park on Route 522. The slat-back chair on the porch was made by a local chair maker.

Hamilton Stillwell poses with a favorite toy for the photographer at Hall Studio in Freehold. In 1992 Hamilton wrote a history of Old Tennent Church from 1890 to 1980.

Eleanor Stillwell enjoys a sunny afternoon in her wicker rocking horse on the porch of the Sutphen-Herbert farmhouse where she was born.

Hamilton and Eleanor are waiting for their sleigh ride to continue after the picture has been taken *c.* 1920.

Charles Wikoff, superintendent of the
Old Tennent Church cemetery from 1939
to 1950, is seen with his wife Jane on a
Sunday afternoon (August 20, 1944).

Charles Wikoff Jr. gives his sister Jane a ride in his Flying Arrow wagon c. 1928.

G. Spafford Reid (1825–1910), a native of the area, resided on a farm on Dey Grove Road. He married Elizabeth Denise Reid in 1851.

Elizabeth Denise Reid (1830–1919) was the wife of G. Spafford Reid.

William H. Reid, the son of G. Spafford and Elizabeth Reid, married Emma Borden Hance Taylor on February 27, 1884, in Holmdel. Emma was the daughter of Michael Taylor, a prominent Monmouth County banker and farmer. William was president of the First National Bank of Englishtown for many years. He served as mayor of Manalapan Township and spent one term in the state assembly. This photograph was taken to celebrate the couples' 40th wedding anniversary.

William H. and Emma T. Reid built this house on Craig Road after their marriage in 1884. Uncharacteristic for the time, the house was designed by Emma and it was built to her specifications. The couple raised six children.

Four generations of the Reid family are represented in this photograph. In the center are G. Spafford and Elizabeth Reid and G. Albert (in the arms of Elizabeth). On the right are G. Albert's parents, George and Emma C. Reid, and on the left are grandparents William H. and Emma T. Reid.

Emma and Hope, daughters-in-law of William and Emma, pretend to take a ride on an early farm sled in the barnyard on Craig Road, but where is the snow?

In 1914 the cows are heading out to the pasture from the William H. Reid farm looking west on Craig Road, after early-morning milking. The milk was taken by wagon to the Tennent railroad station for delivery to a Freehold dairy.

The Reids enjoy a good day of hunting rabbits with their dogs in November of 1912. From left to right are William H. Reid, his son Edgar, grandson Albert, son George, son Henry, son Bill, and an unidentified friend.

Edgar Reid, the son of William H. Reid, married Florence Griffin in 1913 at her home on Huntington, Long Island. Florence came to Tennent to visit her brother and met Edgar when they attended services at Old Tennent Church. After they were married the couple purchased a home and farmlands on Church Lane in Tennent. They raised a son and a daughter.

The home of Edgar and Florence Reid on Church Lane in Tennent appears here.

Leon and Stella Zdancewic moved to their farm on Route 537 in Manalapan Township from Jersey City in 1911. This family photograph was taken around 1920. The oldest boy, Henry, is on the left, followed by mother Stella, son Leon, father Leon, and the youngest son, Edward. Another son, Peter, was born in 1922.

One-year-old Henry Zdancewic is dressed in the child's attire of the period for his photograph in 1912.

The Zdancewic boys, Henry and Leon, are with their friend Ruth in back of the farmhouse. Ruth seems to be enjoying her ride in the potato basket. In the background are a horse trough chiseled from a log, and a few chickens scratching the dirt, a familiar scene on many farms.

In 1924 Henry, Leon, Eddie, Peter, and their friends gathered at the farm on a Sunday afternoon for a pickup game of baseball.

Members of the Zdancewic family—Eddie, Leon, and their parents—proudly show off their new GMC truck, which replaced the horse and wagon for transporting farm produce to market *c.* 1920s.

Father Leon Zdancewic waits patiently for the family to go on a Sunday drive in front of his new Essex automobile *c.* 1925.

In the early spring during the 1930s, Leon and Eddie have returned from a nearby brook with a good catch of pickerel and bass.

Alex and Helen (Zdancewic) Jasko and family are seen after picking apples on their farm on the Englishtown Road about 1925.

Robert T. Blain, proprietor of the woolen mill at Smithburg, appears with his wife, Elizabeth Lefferson Blain, *c.* 1870.

Robert T. Blain appears with his son in front of the Smithburg Mill, which was owned and operated by him from 1866 to 1889.

This photograph taken *c.* 1880 at the Burke Homestead on the corner of Dey and Main Streets in Englishtown Village shows the entire family. From left to right are Mary Ellen, mother Mary (holding Minnie), Carrie, E. Vought Jr., Samuel B., and father Enoch V. Sr.

Enoch Vought Burke Jr., pictured above as a young man, was well known for portraying Uncle Sam in local parades and at patriotic celebrations. No, he is not on stilts; he was 7 feet tall! In the early 1900s he appeared in Washington, D.C., and shook hands with President McKinley.

Samuel Burke, a farmer in Tennent, is shown in his 1915 Model T Ford touring car.

In the summer the car body was removed and a huckster body was placed on the same frame to transport produce to the Freehold market. Note the spare tires tied to the outside of the truck.

The three Rooney brothers, George, Jim and Ed, became owners of Rooney & Ely Co., dealers in feeds, seeds, and farm products in the early 1920s.

The buildings of the Rooney & Ely Co., situated near the railroad tracks in Englishtown, are shown behind George (Bud) and Kathryn Rooney, children of George and Florence Rooney.

An early postcard shows a typical prosperous merchant's home on Main Street in Englishtown in the early 20th century. This home was later owned by Ed Rooney of Rooney & Ely Co.

George Rooney, his wife, Florence, and Jack Crine are standing in front of Ed Rooney's home at 47 Main Street in Englishtown about 1938.

The Cunningham family lived on a farm on Sweetmans Lane near Woodward Road in Manalapan Township. In this 1905 image, Catherine Gleason Cunningham sits on the step, holding a kitten. Catherine's family members are Jane Gleason McCarthy (sister), Mary Gleason (mother), Tom Gleason (brother), Jeremiah Gleason (father), and Mary Ellen Gleason McCarthy (sister).

What is now the Gaitway Horse Farm on Route 33 in Manalapan was originally the Maloney homestead. At one time a room within the farmhouse served as the Peggy Jane Tea Room, pictured on this 1915 postcard. Observe the early ladder-back chairs with rush bottoms, and the windup phonograph.

Ina Huff and a friend are playing with their favorite pets. The wagon was probably made by Ina's father, George Huff, who owned and operated the blacksmith and wheelwright shop at Rue's Corner about 1920.

Harold Snyder, with his horse "Old Mag," uses a Niagara potato duster on the family farm located on Taylor Mills Road c. 1920. No one dusts potatoes wearing a shirt and tie!

The author, who was born in Manalapan Township, enjoys a day of fishing with his father, Joseph, at the Smithburg millpond in 1940. Young Richard never went anywhere without his toy gun!

Fairview Farms, owned by Gus and Constance Dreyer, was located on the Freehold-Englishtown Road across from Taylor Mills Road. In 1943 the Dreyer children, Mary Ann, Marjorie, and Gus, are waiting for a ride in Dad's truck.

Five

Homes

The Captain John Anderson House, built c. 1700, was located on Highway 33 near Manalapan Village and is no longer standing. Captain Anderson was a veteran of the ill-fated Darien Expedition that tried to colonize Panama for Scotland. The expedition failed because of disease and a lack of supplies from Scotland. Three ships tried to return to Scotland. One made it there, another shipwrecked at sea, and the third, captained by Anderson, made it to New Jersey.

This land was originally owned by John Reid, who received it in exchange for his work as surveyor general of East Jersey. When Reid's daughter Anna married Capt. John Anderson, John Reid gave them the property as a wedding gift. The house was built sometime prior to 1709 and is representative of early-18th-century construction. The exterior was furnished partly with round-end, hand-split shingles and partly with beaded clapboard. The original smaller portion was followed by larger two-story additions made in 1730 and 1750. The house included slave quarters, an early Dutch oven, five fireplaces on the first floor, and hand-blown glass windowpanes.

One of the earliest homes in the township was built by Cornelius Thompson in 1702 on land that was originally part of the tract known as the Passaguanacua Indian Purchase about 1690. The Thompson farm, originally encompassing 3,000 acres, was located near the Burlington Path between Smithburg and Freehold. The house was of stone structure with walls 2 feet thick, ceilings of clear yellow pine, and an iron latch on the door marked with "CET 1702." This inscription represented the initials of Cornelius and his wife, Elizabeth Almy Morris, daughter of Lewis Morris. Members of the Thompson family resided on a portion of the farm until 1844. Other owners included Hendrickson, Hartman, and Clayton. Speculators owned the property when the house burned in late 1965.

The Reuben Dorrer house, built c. 1840, was constructed on a portion of the original Cornelius Thompson farm. John Ely bought the property from Thomas Thompson, a descendant of Cornelius, in 1836. Later owners were Jacob Pittenger, Clark Clayton, and Garret Hartman. Mr. Dorrer operated the farm from 1927 until his death in 1987.

The Zdancewic house, known as Wood-Z-Lane Farm on Route 537, was marked by the Battleground Historical Society as having been built *c.* 1840. It was also built on part of the 3,000-acre Cornelius Thompson farm that was later broken up into 100-acre lots. Robert James bought this portion of the farm, which was later owned by Tunis DuBois. DuBois's granddaughter inherited the property from her father, Benjamin DuBois, and deeded it to Stella Zdancewic.

This early dwelling, built *c.* 1770 on Locust Hill, part of the 1,000-acre Capt. John Anderson tract, was located on LeValley Road. It has been traced back to John and Elias Covenhaven. J. VanDoren is shown as the owner in the 1873 *Beers' Atlas*. Today the property is a Boy Scout reservation known as Quail Hill.

Floral Hall, built *c*. 1820, was located on the James M. Perrine farm on the Manalapan-Freehold Turnpike, now Highway 33. It was used by the Knob Hill Country Club until it was replaced by a modern housing development.

Four generations of the Probasco family have lived in this lovely old farmhouse near Millhurst, built *c*. 1833. An early photograph shows the picket fence and yard just as it is now. The original owner was William I. Conover. It remained in the Conover family until 1869. The DuBois family lived in the house until it was sold to Tunis D. Probasco in 1909.

The Orr House, built c. 1780, was purchased by Thomas Orr in 1904. The foundation stone is thought to be from a ship's ballast. The cellar steps are made of heavy flagstone. Bark-covered oak beams remain under the main portion of the house. One huge log runs from the cellar to the peak of the roof. Early owners were Asher Ely, Bowne Reid, and T. Smith.

This lovely Victorian mansion known as the VanNest-DuBois house was built c. 1870. Research indicates that the lower part is older. It was located on Symmes Road near the Monmouth County Library.

Gordon's Tavern, located on a high elevation overlooking Highway 9, was marked as having been built c. 1797 because of a deed to Daniel Gordon on record in Freehold for the Gordons Corner property on Gravelly Hill Road. This road no longer exists. Just when the tavern was built is not known. The small section at the back of the house was the original tavern with a bar in the corner. The original glass windows still exist. The settlement of Gordon's estate in 1819 included the contents of the tavern. Capt. David Gordon of Revolutionary fame lived in the house at one time.

The David Forman house, built c. 1737, is located in the Covered Bridge Development on Route 9. General Forman, also known as Devil Dave, commanded the New Jersey State Militia and originated Washington's Intelligence Service during the Revolutionary War. He was known for his bravery and daring.

94

Charles and Lydia Wikoff purchased the farmstead on Tennent Road near Gordons Corner from Jesse Boyce in 1952. The lovely two-story colonial was built *c.* 1851.

The Conover homestead on Gordons Corner Road near Conmack Lane was purchased by Garret B. Conover *c.* 1835. Mr. Conover was a prosperous farmer and served as an elder at Old Tennent Church. He married Teresa, daughter of James I. Reid, and the couple had seven children. This house remained in the Conover family for many generations.

Dr. James English, a Revolutionary War surgeon, lived in this house built *c.* 1740, and was said to have entertained George Washington. The house is located on Gordons Corner Road across from the Taylor Mills School, and is in excellent repair and surrounded by beautiful old boxwood trees. Dr. English married Hannah Perrine and had seven children.

This house was built in 1851 for James English, grandson of Dr. James English. The construction date appears on two sides under the eves. The farmhouse still stands next to the Taylor Mills School. It became the Aumack Dairy in 1878, beginning with 20 cows and growing to 125 cows in 1959. Miss Madelyn Aumack remembers her grandfather delivering milk to local residents in Englishtown.

The Dreyer house, located on the Tennent-Englishtown Road opposite Taylor Mills Road, was constructed c. 1845 for the Rev. L.H. VanDoren, pastor of the Old Tennent Church (1840–56). Joseph H. VanMater purchased the property in 1856. The initials "JHVM" are scratched on a windowpane. In 1889 John H. Laird was listed as the owner in Wolverton's *Atlas of Monmouth County*. The Dreyer family purchased the property from Arthur Brokaw in 1926. It was used as a cattle farm by Clayton Palmer until 1937, when Gustav and Constance Dreyer were married. They operated a truck farm, producing vegetables to be sold at local markets, until 1977. The property is now part of the Manalapan Township Recreation Park. The millstone from Taylor's Mill was found on the farm and is displayed at the Taylor Mills School on Gordon's Corner Road.

This dwelling located on Iron Ore Road, built c. 1839, is on the site of the Aaron L. Reid homestead of 1775. The house was in the Reid family for many generations and descendants still live in the area. Supporting beams under one section are actually made from trees split in half and still covered with bark. A main beam, hewn from one large tree, goes from cellar to attic. The Palmer family purchased the property in 1957, originally as a cattle farm. It is now a horse breeding farm known as Boxwood Farm.

The Cobb House located on Route 522 was built by Rev. Archibald Cobb in 1870. It replaced an earlier house on the property known as Roy Parsonage, which burned to the ground on a Sunday afternoon in 1869. Reverend Cobb was the 12th pastor of the Old Tennent Church from August 8, 1863, until his death on February 26, 1881. The Cobb House, located on the Monmouth Battlefield State Park, is now used as headquarters for New Jersey Region 2 of the park system.

The carriage barn behind the Cobb House follows the same architectural design as the house.

Chrineyonce VanMater and his wife, Linda, were the original owners of the house located at 17 Tennent Avenue in Englishtown, built c. 1850. In 1859 they sold it to John I. Emmons.

William Hess, a previous owner of this c. 1848 house, ran a tavern in the building later purchased by the borough for offices and a firehouse. This was also the home of Edna Hamilton. The Hamilton family owned the drugstore on the corner of Main and Mechanic Streets in the early 20th century.

In the early 19th century the Laird family owned large tracts of land in Englishtown, as well as houses and stores. Early maps show David Laird residing in this house on Water Street, built c. 1730. The similarity of this house to the Village Inn nearby indicates they were built in the same era. A later resident was Jacob Burke, a local blacksmith. The house is no longer standing.

The Cornelius Applegate homestead on Tracy Station Road, built c. 1847, is now owned by his great-granddaughter, Alma Grove. Her father, James R. Lutes, was a farmer and a tinsmith.

The tinsmith shop run by James R. Lutes provided items such as candle molds, sconces, and kitchen utensils for the home. The workshop and tools were donated to the New Jersey Museum of Agriculture in New Brunswick in 1985.

The Pinelands, shown on a 1910 postcard, was also known as Westerfeld's Boarding House. It was a summer boarding home located on Pension Road. There was also a cider mill on the property. Women and children came to the Pinelands from New York City to escape the heat and enjoy fresh country air. Their husbands joined them on the weekend. The building burned in the 1930s.

Long's House and Lake, Englishtown, N. J.

Long's Boarding House and Lake were located on Union Hill Road, a short distance off of the Englishtown-Old Bridge Road. In 1911 families from New York City, Newark, and Jersey City arrived at the Englishtown train station to spend a summer vacation at the local boarding houses.

A 1930s postcard shows visitors enjoying a summer day on the porch at Long's Boarding House.

Six

Churches and Schools

The congregation of the Old Tennent Church was organized in 1692 as the Old Scots Church. The present church was built in 1751 on 1 acre of land purchased from William Ker for 1 shilling 20 years earlier. John Davis was the chief carpenter. The church was originally planned on a lower part of White Hill, and tradition has it that Janet Rhea, a church member, seized the small cornerstone in her apron and struggled to the top of the hill, telling everyone that she wanted to go up to the house of the Lord.

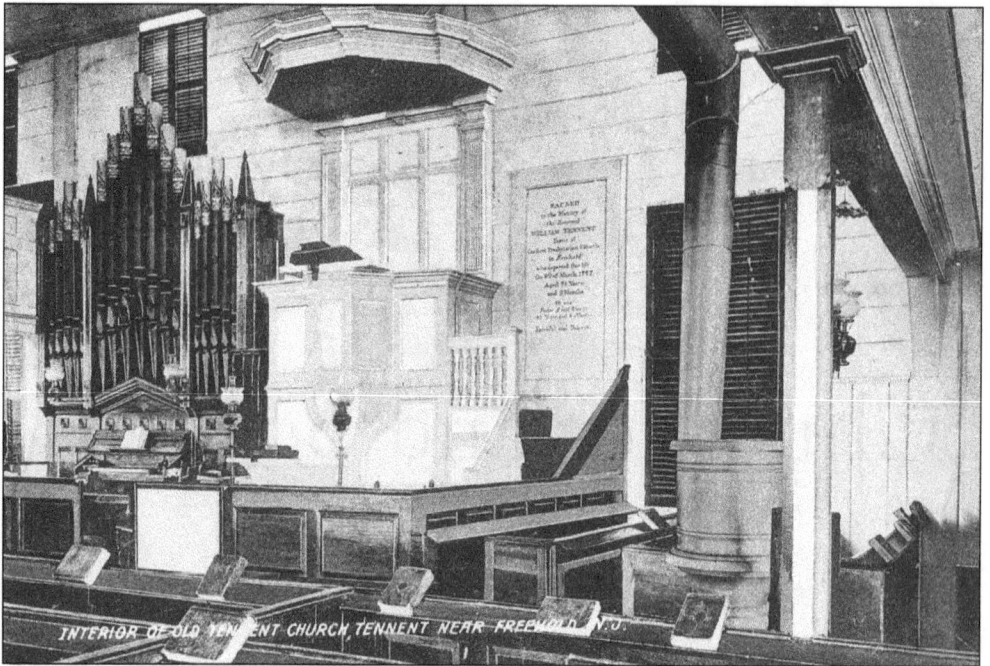

INTERIOR OF OLD TENNENT CHURCH TENNENT NEAR FREEHOLD N.J.

There was no heat in the interior of the Old Tennent Church until four stoves were added about 1815. Women worshippers often used foot warmers consisting of a wooden box lined with tin and filled with live coals. The pipe organ, built by M.P. Moller of Hagerstown, Maryland, and set into a recess constructed for it, was used for the first time on Sunday, December 14, 1890. J. Chalmers Rue was the organist. Gas lamps were installed in 1913 and used until 1949.

Goodwin's Marching Band from Cranbury, New Jersey, is shown in front of the Old Tennent Church c. 1925. The band provided music for the annual harvest home festival held each summer at the church. People came from miles around to have a good time and enjoy a country supper for only 35¢. The 4:30 p.m. train arrived at the Tennent railroad station with large containers of the famous Day's ice cream from Ocean Grove, New Jersey.

Rev. Frank R. Symmes was installed as the 15th pastor of the Old Tennent Church on February 18, 1890, and served the congregation for 29 years. Reverend Symmes was a graduate of Princeton University and the Princeton Theological Seminary. In 1904 he published the *History of the Old Tennent Church*, which included a large collection of genealogical notes.

This early farmhouse, built *c*. 1791 and now known as Cannon Hill on Main Street in Tennent, was the home of the pastors of the Old Tennent Church from 1881 to 1952. Rev. Charles H. Neff, pastor from 1926 to 1963, lived here until the new manse was completed.

To celebrate the bicentennial of the church building, in 1951 a historical pageant was presented by members dressed in period costume. Emil Menzel, Charles Wikoff, Theodore Griewe, and Duncan Perrine are shown with the collection poles used during the 18th century.

The cemetery surrounding the Old Tennent Church began on 1 acre of land and has grown to 72 acres. Records indicate that 110 veterans of the Revolution are buried in this cemetery. The oldest stone is for Robert Rhea, who died in 1720.

The Englishtown Presbyterian Church, a branch of the Old Tennent Church organization, was formed in 1860 to accommodate members living in the village. The building, located on north Main Street, was built the same year. In 1876 members severed their connection with the Old Tennent Church and secured the services of Rev. Donald McLaren.

The Presbyterian parsonage, located on the north corner of Main and Center Streets, is shown here on a 1930s postcard.

The Sanford Memorial Church, formerly known as the Methodist Episcopal Church, located on South Main Street in Englishtown, was organized in 1842 in the old schoolhouse. This building was dedicated on October 10, 1878, and the first pastor was the Reverend Robert J. Andrews. Early trustees were J.O. Burtt, Elisha McCabe, Simeon Pettit, Daniel Sanford, and Gilbert Applegate. About 1905 philanthropist Charles Sanford provided funds to renovate the church, build a parsonage, and establish a public library for the community.

Interior of Sanford Public Library, Sanford Memorial M. E. Church, Englishtown, N. J.

This is the interior of the Sanford Public Library located in the Sanford Memorial Methodist Episcopal Church. An early radiator kept the members warm.

108

Our Lady of Mercy Roman Catholic Church, located on the north corner of Main Street and Pine Street, was built in 1948. Prior to the completion of the building, services were held in the Noce home across the street and in the Englishtown Municipal Building.

The rectory for Our Lady of Mercy Roman Catholic Church was purchased c. 1948 and is located next to the church on the south corner of Main and Center Streets. The first priest was Father Nolan.

The first Jewish synagogue in the area was located on Mechanic Street (now Hamilton Street) in Englishtown Borough. It was built in 1919 and Rabbi Morris Zarchin was the leader of the congregation that began in 1917.

The St. James African Methodist Episcopal Church, located on Smithburg Road north of Sweetman's Lane, was established about 1836 by freed black slaves, and incorporated on August 9, 1843. An early deed indicates the property was sold to the congregation for $23.60 on August 18, 1846, by Lewis I. Conover and his wife, Catherine, former slaves. It is the second oldest active church in the township and surrounded by an early burial ground.

The Manalapan Presbyterian Church, located on the corner of Route 33 and Conover Road, is no longer standing. The cornerstone was laid on October 10, 1855, and the new building dedicated on July 31, 1856. On that date the church was officially organized; the first minister, Rev. John L. Kehoo, was installed on June 30, 1857.

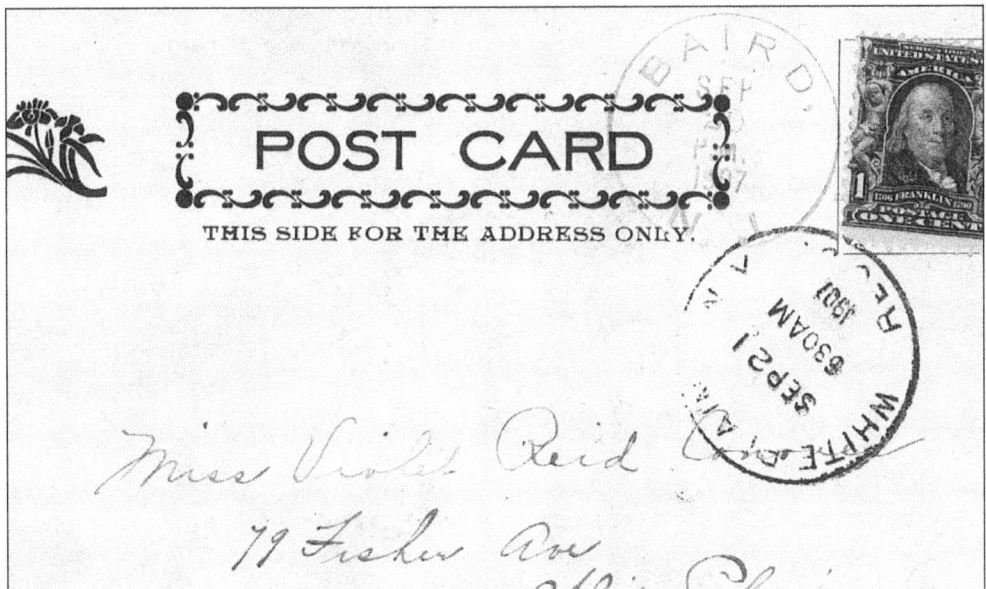

The reverse side of this Manalapan Presbyterian Church postcard has a rare 1907 Baird, New Jersey, cancellation. The post office was located in a small general store on Baird Road near the church. It operated there from April 17, 1897, until March 31, 1909. The postmistress was Emma R. Baird. The back of the card was used for address only until 1908. This card left the area via the railroad sometime after noon on September 20, 1907, and arrived in White Plains, New York, at 6:30 a.m. on September 21, 1907!

In 1920 students from Manalapan and Freehold Townships attended the Thompson Grove School, which was built c. 1845 just north of Route 537 on Thompson Grove Road on part of the original Cornelius Thompson 3,000-acre plantation. The one-room schoolhouse, which is no longer standing, was used until 1936 and some local residents who attended the school still live in the area.

The Blacks Mills School was built after 1855 on property owned by James Showles on the Manalapan Road (now Route 33 in Millhurst) and moved to an adjoining lot in 1864. It was later used as a home, and now has been replaced by a modern car wash. Miss Marion Symmes, daughter of Rev. Frank Symmes, was a teacher at the school early in her career in the 1920s.

Early maps show a schoolhouse located in the village of Manalapan. A c. 1906 postcard shows children and their teacher in front of the Manalapan School, also known as Bergen Mills School.

In the fall of 1922, children of all ages were taught at the one-room schoolhouse in Manalapan by Miss Mary Orr.

The Vanderveer School began with a small group of children attending at Dr. John T. Woodhull's carriage house. About 1830 the parents united and built a schoolhouse on the Woodhull farm, located on the north side of Manalapan Road. No deed was given and the schoolhouse was later sold with the farm. In 1840, the schoolhouse shown in this photograph was built on property purchased from Major John Perrine. The first teacher was Miss Ellen Shaw.

Mamie Rue is shown with her pupils at the Vanderveer School c. 1897. Carl Woodward, age 7, who was a teacher in the Lafayette School in 1909, is in the front row on the left. His brother Howard, who was mayor of Manalapan Township (1943–47), is also in the photograph.

The public school in Tennent was erected in 1863 across from the Old Tennent Church. It is still standing as a private residence.

Children who attended the public school in Tennent sat at double desks and paid strict attention to their teacher, Eleanor Snyder Griswold, c. 1915.

These students are proud of the new Lafayette School, which was built in 1915, replacing the earlier school built in 1860.

A school photograph taken in 1909 shows teacher Carl Woodward with his students in front of the early Lafayette School.

The public school on the corner of Main and Pine Streets in Englishtown was built in 1909. Directly behind this building the Pine Street School was built in 1930 to accommodate the growing population of the Manalapan-Englishtown area. In 1983 it was sold to the Freehold Regional High School District for administrative offices. The original school serves as offices for the Manalapan Township Board of Education.

Eleanor Snyder, a native of Manalapan Township, graduated from Freehold High School in the spring of 1910. She is the fourth person from the left in the top row. In the fall of 1910 she began her teaching career at the one-room Lafayette School. Eleanor later taught at the Tennent School before moving to the Pine Street School in Englishtown Borough in 1935 to teach second grade. She eventually became the principal and retired in 1956.

In 1952, 50 eighth-grade students from Manalapan and Englishtown prepared for graduation at the Main Street Public School. The faculty in photograph are George Miller (superintendent), Erma Dorrer (principal and eighth-grade teacher), and Mrs. N. Vanderhoeff (eighth-grade teacher). This was the first class to be divided by locality between Jamesburg High School and Freehold High School.

Lydia Wikoff, Manalapan Township historian, has been instrumental in naming the modern schools after early mills and brooks. She is especially proud of the millstone from Taylor's Mill found on the Gus Dreyer farm, which has been donated by the Dreyers to the school.

Seven

Military History

In the mid-18th century Thomas Davis and his son Moses lived, worked, and kept a tavern in this house in Englishtown. Moses Davis, a lieutenant in the Monmouth County Militia, died in March 1777. The new owner, Daniel Herbert, may have leased the building as a residence until he began keeping the tavern here in 1779. Before and after the Battle of Monmouth, the building probably served as an officer's quarters. Major portions of the Continental Army encamped nearby on June 27, 1778. Surgeon Samuel Adams of the 3rd Continental Artillery wrote, "this place which is a small village of six or eight houses takes its name of Englishtown from three Irishmen of the name of English that first settled here, is no agreeable situation, the ground being rather low and the air much confined by the surrounding woods."

The Old Revolutionary Church was drawn and engraved by J. Smillie. Constructed between 1751 and 1753, the New Presbyterian Meeting House on White Oak Hill was a prominent landmark at a strategic road intersection between Englishtown and Monmouth Courthouse. The Hunterdon and Somerset County Militia were headquartered here before the battle; during and after the battle the Continental Army used the building as a field hospital.

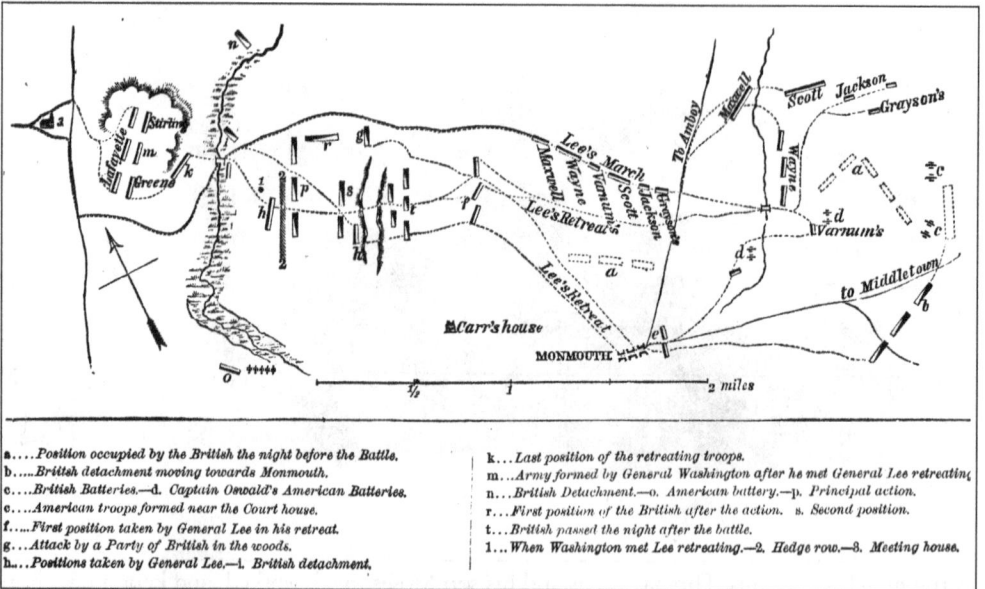

a....Position occupied by the British the night before the Battle.
b.....British detachment moving towards Monmouth.
c....British Batteries.—d. Captain Onwald's American Batteries.
e....American troops formed near the Court house.
f.....First position taken by General Lee in his retreat.
g...Attack by a Party of British in the woods.
h...Positions taken by General Lee.—i. British detachment.

k...Last position of the retreating troops.
m...Army formed by General Washington after he met General Lee retreating
n....British Detachment.—o. American battery.—p. Principal action.
r...First position of the British after the action. s. Second position.
t...British passed the night after the battle.
1...When Washington met Lee retreating.—2. Hedge row.—3. Meeting house.

This 19th-century map of the Battle of Monmouth is a simplification of the 1778 plan drawn by Michel Captaine du Chesnoy, cartographer to the Marquis de Lafayette. The battle began when Maj. Gen. Charles Lee led an advance force of Continentals from Englishtown past the Presbyterian Meeting House (3) to the outskirts of Monmouth Courthouse. There he attempted to surround the British rear guard (b-c). When the British attacked with their entire first division, Lee was forced to retreat (e-f). Near (s) (not 1), Lee met Washington and at his direction began fighting a delaying action (g-h). Washington arrayed the main body of the Continental Army on the hill east of the meetinghouse.

120

A modern reconstruction of the battlefield illustrates the farms along the Freehold-Englishtown Road. The area corresponds to the western portion of the Michel Captaine du Chesnoy map.

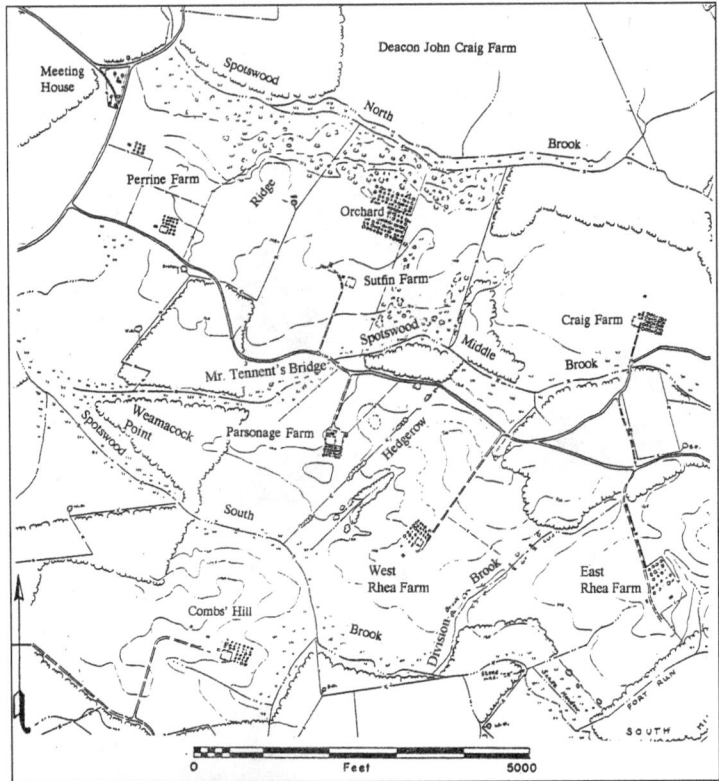

Brig. Gen. David Forman (1745–1797), the ambitious and ruthless leader of Monmouth County's Whigs, lived 5 miles north of Monmouth Courthouse at Matchaponax. A loyalist foraging party raided Forman's plantation on June 27th, but the group was driven back to Monmouth Courthouse by the New Jersey Militia. On June 28, Forman helped guide Maj. Gen. Charles Lee's advance forces during their attempt to outflank the British rear guard. (Painting by Charles Willson Peale.)

121

WASHINGTON AND LEE AT MONMOUTH.

This is a 19th-century view of Lee meeting Washington on the Rhea plantations just west of Division Brook. Washington directed Wayne and Lee to fight a delaying action while Washington returned to the Perrine Farm to organize a defensive line. While Washington was angry with Lee, the story of his swearing at Lee "till the leaves shook on the trees" is a 19th-century fiction. Washington's break with Lee and Lee's court-martial were engineered by Washington's aides after the battle.

Molly Pitcher at the Battle of Monmouth is an 1858 engraving by J. Rogers from a painting by Dennis Malone Carter. After the British grenadier charge toward "Mr. Tennent's Bridge" collapsed, the battle evolved into a long-range artillery duel between 10 British guns along the hedgerow and 10 or 12 Continental guns on the Perrine Ridge. The Continental Army was arrayed in three or four well-spaced lines—skirmishers along the fence between the Perrine and Sutfin Farms, the artillery on the hill side, the main body of infantry on the military crest, and the reserves behind the crest. Mary Hays was the wife of a gunner in the Pennsylvania artillery regiment. After heat stroke or British artillery fire decimated her husband's gun crew, Molly volunteered to help work the gun. During the 19th century, memories of this plucky Irish girl evolved into patriotic myth.

The Battle of Monmouth is an 1868 engraving from a painting by Alonzo Chappel. The view is north-northeast, with the buildings of the Presbyterian parsonage at the left. Adapting Benson Lossing's 1850 *View of the Battle-ground at Monmouth*, Chappel has painted two elements of the battle. In the foreground is the last action of the battle—the late afternoon attack by Brig. Gen. Anthony Wayne on the retreating first battalion of British grenadiers. In the background is the next-to-last element of the morning retreat—the storming of the hedgerow by the second battalion of British grenadiers.

The Bivouac at Monmouth is an 1856 engraving by J.C. Buttre from a painting by Alonzo Chappel. The battle ended in late afternoon, when the British pulled back to the east Rhea farm. The exhausted Continentals slept on their arms, intending to resume the battle in the morning, but daybreak revealed that the British had retreated to Middletown. Washington, his "family" of aides, and the Marquis de Lafayette spent the night under a large tree on the Perrine or Sutfin farm, their only bedding the cloak that Washington spread on the ground.

123

At the west end of the Presbyterian Meeting House (now the Old Tennent Church) is the grave of Lt. Col. Henry Monckton, commander of the second battalion of British grenadiers, killed by a blast of grapeshot as Continental guns raked the approaches to "Mr. Tennent's Bridge." To the north of Monckton's grave is a memorial to Capt. Henry Fauntleroy, 5th Virginia, an officer in one of the Continental battalions of "picked men" of Maj. Gen. Lee's advanced force.

The dwelling house of the Parsonage Farm was from 1732 to 1777 the home of the Reverend William Tennent, a prominent supporter of the Great Awakening. In the last phase of the 1778 battle, Brig. Gen. Anthony Wayne and three regiments of Pennsylvanians took cover in the parsonage barn, dwelling, and orchard as they held off a counterattack by the first battalion of British grenadiers. This postcard illustrates the parsonage shortly before its demolition in 1860. Note the long shingles and brick insulation of the Dutch-framed dwelling. The kitchen wing dates from the early 19th century.

The Sutfin Farm looking north from the Freehold-Englishtown Road was realigned in 1820. To the right in a grove of elm trees is the dwelling, the oldest portion dating from the 1730s. During the battle, this was a no-man's-land between the two armies. The Sutfins returned to find the house plundered. Derick Sutfin's three youngest sons were on the Manasquan River with the Monmouth County Militia and Morgan's Rifle Brigade. Militia and riflemen harassed the British encampment at Monmouth Courthouse, capturing 15 grenadiers washing their clothes in a brook.

This is Spotswood Middle Brook looking north towards the site of "Mr. Tennent's Bridge." To the right is the Parsonage Farm to the left is the Sutfin Farm. This view shows the brook after it was ditched in the 19th century. Before the brook was deepened, the meadow to the left was a bushy marsh obstructing the movements of formed troops. The postcard caption is an exaggeration. This card is one of a c. 1915 series illustrating the battlefield. Note the late-19th-century tenant house of the Thompson-Taylor farm.

This view is from the Parsonage Farm looking north-northwest across Spotswood Middle Brook into the Sutfin Farm. During the battle, a corner of a parsonage wood lot blocked this sight line, partially screening the two armies from each other. Washington met Lee one-half mile further east. To the left, note the Thompson-Taylor tenant house and the photographer's car.

MOLLIE PITCHER'S WELL, FREEHOLD, N. J.

Molly Pitcher's Well is a fiction invented for the convenience of railroad passengers, but in the background of this image is the Thompson-Taylor farm created in 1837 by combining portions of the Sutfin, Parsonage, and Rhea Farms. Some of the oak trees in the barnyard may be relics of the parsonage wood lot. The view is looking north. During the battle, the hedgerow fence ran diagonally across this view, from the lower left to the upper right. The British grenadiers and guardsmen pushed across this area as they drove Lee's advance force back over the bridge.

126

Maj. Peter Vrendenberg Jr. of Freehold, the oldest son of Judge Peter Vrendenberg, was the commanding officer of the 14th New Jersey Voluntary Infantry Regiment during the Civil War. He was killed in the charge at Opequan, Virginia, on September 19, 1864. The 14th New Jersey Voluntary Infantry Regiment was organized at Camp Vrendenberg in 1862. The camp was located in Manalapan Township behind the Cobb House on Route 522, on land where Continental soldiers had fought for independence in 1778.

James R. Lutes was enrolled in Company A of the 14th New Jersey Voluntary Infantry Regiment in August 1862 at Camp Vrendenberg, and discharged on June 18, 1865.

Isaac N. Ker, the great-great grandson of Walter Ker, an early settler and landowner in Tennent, was at Camp Vrendenberg in 1862 and served as a fifer until July 6, 1863.

Isaac's brother, William H. Ker, was a drummer boy in Company A of the 28th Regiment of the New Jersey Voluntary Infantry in 1862 at the age of 14 years. The boys' grandfather, Ebenezer Ker, served in the Revolutionary War from 1775 to 1783.

www.ingramcontent.com/pod-product-compliance
Lightning Source LLC
Chambersburg PA
CBHW080901100426
42812CB00007B/2115